Quick & Easy Mittens

Choose from 9 sizes to make mittens for everyone! Easy instructions and photos guide you in knitting with two traditional needles or the Knook®

LEISURE ARTS, INC.
Maumelle, Arkansas

Mittens

EASY

SHOPPING LIST

Yarn (Medium Weight)

MEDIUM 4

[7 ounces, 364 yards (198 grams, 333 meters) per skein]:

- ☐ {65-65-80}{100-115-135}{145-165-180} yards/{59.5-59.5-73}{91-105-123}{133-151-165} meters

Note: Yarn amounts are given for the **total** amount needed for a pair of mittens. When making any of the variations, divide this amount between the colors used accordingly.

Knitting Needles

Straight needles,

- ☐ Size 5 (3.75 mm) **and**
- ☐ Size 7 (4.5 mm)

or sizes needed for gauge

OR

Knooks

- ☐ Size G (4 mm) **and**
- ☐ Size H (5 mm)

or sizes needed for gauge

Additional Supplies

- ☐ Stitch holder - 2
- ☐ Split-ring marker - 2
- ☐ Yarn needle

SIZE INFORMATION

Selecting Correct Size Mitten:

Size indicates the number of inches (centimeters) around the palm, measured just above the thumb.

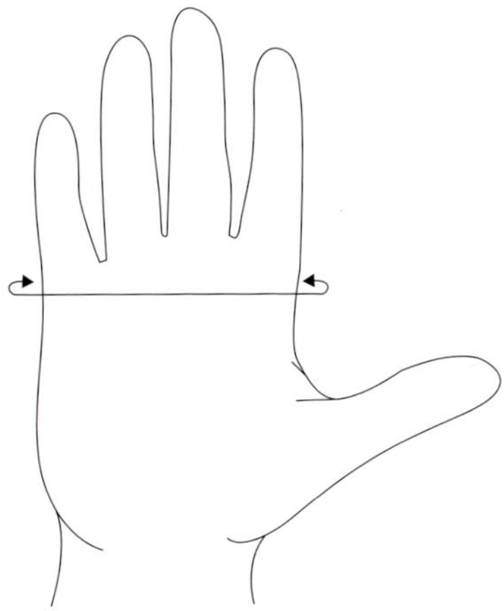

Size Note: We have printed the sizes in colors to make it easier for you to find:

- Size 5" (12.5 cm) in Blue
- Size 5½" (14 cm) in Pink
- Size 6" (15 cm) in Green
- Size 6½" (16.5 cm) in Purple
- Size 7" (18 cm) in Olive
- Size 7½" (19 cm) in Navy
- Size 8" (20.5 cm) in Brown
- Size 8½" (21.5 cm) in Red
- Size 9" (23 cm) in Yellow

Instructions in Black apply to all sizes.

Knit Instructions

GAUGE INFORMATION

See Gauge on page 31.

With larger size needles, in Stockinette Stitch

(knit one row, purl one row), 20 sts and 28 rows = 4" (10 cm)

TECHNIQUES USED

- Markers ***(see Markers, page 31)***
- Knit Increase ***(Figs. 1a & b, page 34)***
- Adding new stitches ***(Figs. 2a & b, page 34)***
- K2 tog ***(Fig. 3, page 35)***
- Slip 1, K1, PSSO ***(Figs. 4a & b, page 35)***

See Changing Colors (Figs. A & B, page 20).

Ribbing

With smaller size needles, cast on {23-25-27}{29-31-33}{35-37-39} sts **loosely**.

Row 1: P1, (K1, P1) across.

Row 2 (Right side)**:** K1, (P1, K1) across.

Repeat Rows 1 and 2 until Ribbing measures approximately {2-2½-2½}{2¾-3-3}{3¼-3¼-3½}"/{5-6.5-6.5}{7-7.5-7.5}{8.5-8.5-9} cm from cast on edge, ending by working Row 1.

Body

Change to larger size needles.

Row 1: Knit across increasing {5-5-5}{5-7-7}{7-9-9} sts evenly spaced ***(see Increasing Evenly Across a Row, page 33)***: {28-30-32}{34-38-40}{42-46-48} sts.

Row 2: Purl across.

Sizes 8, 8½, and 9 Only - Rows 3 and 4: Work across in Stockinette Stitch.

SHAPING (All Sizes)

Row 1: Knit {13-14-15}{16-18-19}{20-22-23} sts, place marker, increase twice, place marker, knit across: {30-32-34}{36-40-42}{44-48-50} sts.

Row 2: Purl across.

Row 3 (Increase row): Knit across to next marker, increase, knit to within one st of next marker, increase, knit across: {32-34-36}{38-42-44}{46-50-52} sts.

Repeat Rows 2 and 3, {1-2-2}{3-3-4}{4-5-5} time(s): {34-38-40}{44-48-52}{54-60-62} sts.

Work even in Stockinette Stitch until Mitten measures approximately {3¼-4-4}{4¾-5-5¼}{5¾-6-6¼}"/{8.5-10-10}{12-12.5-13.5}{14.5-15-16} cm from cast on edge, ending by working a **purl** row.

Thumb

Row 1: Knit across to next marker and slip these {13-14-15}{16-18-19}{20-22-23} sts just worked onto st holder, remove marker, add on one st; knit added on st, knit across to next marker, remove marker, **turn**; add on one st, slip remaining sts onto second st holder: {10-12-12}{14-14-16}{16-18-18} sts.

Work even until Thumb measures approximately {1¼-1½-1¾}{2-2¼-2½}{2½-2¾-2¾}"/{3-4-4.5}{5-5.5-6.5}{6.5-7-7} cm, ending by working a **purl** row.

Next Row: K2 tog across: {5-6-6}{7-7-8}{8-9-9} sts.

Cut yarn leaving a long end.

Thread yarn needle with end and slip remaining stitches from knitting needle onto yarn needle; gather stitches **tightly** to close, then secure end; do **not** cut yarn. With same yarn weave seam ***(Fig. 9, page 38)***.

Hand

With **right** side facing, slip sts from first st holder onto needle; with same needle, pick up a st in each of 2 added on sts; slip sts from second st holder onto empty needle and knit across: {28-30-32}{34-38-40}{42-46-48} sts.

Work even until piece measures approximately {4¾-6-6}{7-7½-7¾}{8½-8¾-9¼}"/{12-15-15}{18-19-19.5}{21.5-22-23.5} cm from cast on edge, ending by working a **knit** row.

Next Row: Purl {14-15-16} {17-19-20}{21-23-24} sts, place marker, purl across.

SHAPING

Row 1: K2, slip 1 as if to **knit**, K1, PSSO, knit across to within 3 sts of marker, K2 tog, K1, slip marker, K1, slip 1 as if to **knit**, K1, PSSO, knit across to last 4 sts, K2 tog, K2: {24-26-28}{30-34-36}{38-42-44} sts.

Row 2: Purl across.

Repeat Rows 1 and 2, {1-2-3} {3-4-5}{5-5-5} time(s): {20-18-16} {18-18-16}{18-22-24} sts.

Next Row: K2 tog across: {10-9-8} {9-9-8}{9-11-12} sts.

Cut yarn leaving a long end.

Thread yarn needle with end and slip remaining stitches from knitting needle onto yarn needle; gather stitches **tightly** to close, then secure end. Weave seam.

Weave in yarn ends ***(Fig. 10, page 38)***.

Knook Instructions

GAUGE INFORMATION

See Gauge on page 31.

With larger size Knook, in Stockinette Stitch (knit one row, purl one row), 20 sts and 28 rows = 4" (10 cm)

TECHNIQUES USED

- Markers ***(see Markers, page 31)***
- Knit Increase ***(Figs. 5a & b, page 36)***
- M1 ***(Figs. 6a & b, page 36)***
- K2 tog ***(Figs. 7a & b, page 37)***
- Slip 1, K1, PSSO ***(Figs. 8a & b, page 37)***

See Changing Colors (Figs. A & B, page 20).

Ribbing

With smaller size Knook, ch {23-25-27}{29-31-33}{35-37-39}.

Foundation Row (Right side)**:** Pick up {22-24-26}{28-30-32}{34-36-38} sts on foundation ch: {23-25-27}{29-31-33}{35-37-39} sts.

Row 1: P1, (K1, P1) across.

Row 2 (Right side)**:** K1, (P1, K1) across.

Repeat Rows 1 and 2 until Ribbing measures approximately {2-2½-2½}{2¾-3-3}{3¼-3¼-3½}"/{5-6.5-6.5}{7-7.5-7.5}{8.5-8.5-9} cm from foundation ch edge, ending by working Row 1.

Body

Change to larger size Knook.

Row 1: Knit across increasing {5-5-5}{5-7-7}{7-9-9} sts evenly spaced ***(see Increasing Evenly Across a Row, page 33)***: {28-30-32}{34-38-40}{42-46-48} sts.

Row 2: Purl across.

Sizes 8, 8½, and 9 Only - Rows 3 and 4: Work across in Stockinette Stitch.

SHAPING (All Sizes)

Row 1: Knit {13-14-15}{16-18-19}{20-22-23} sts, place marker, increase twice, place marker, knit across: {30-32-34}{36-40-42}{44-48-50} sts.

Row 2: Purl across.

Row 3 (Increase row)**:** Knit across to next marker, increase, knit to within one st of next marker, increase, knit across: {32-34-36}{38-42-44}{46-50-52} sts.

Repeat Rows 2 and 3, {1-2-2}{3-3-4}{4-5-5} time(s): {34-38-40}{44-48-52}{54-60-62} sts.

Work even in Stockinette Stitch until Mitten measures approximately {3¼-4-4}{4¾-5-5¼}{5¾-6-6¼}"/{8.5-10-10}{12-12.5-13.5}{14.5-15-16} cm from foundation ch edge, ending by working a **purl** row.

Thumb

Row 1: Knit across to next marker, unthread Knook leaving sts on cord, thread Knook with second cord, M1, remove marker and place marker in same strand, knit across to next marker, M1, remove marker and place marker in same strand, **turn**; leave remaining sts on cord: {10-12-12}{14-14-16}{16-18-18} sts.

Work even until Thumb measures approximately {1¼-1½-1¾}{2-2¼-2½}{2½-2¾-2¾}"/{3-4-4.5}{5-5.5-6.5}{6.5-7-7} cm, ending by working a **purl** row.

Next Row: K2 tog across: {5-6-6}{7-7-8}{8-9-9} sts.

Cut yarn leaving a long end.

Thread yarn needle with end and slip remaining stitches from cord onto yarn needle; gather the stitches **tightly** to close, then secure end; do **not** cut yarn. With same yarn weave seam *(Fig. 9, page 38)*.

Hand

With **right** side facing, thread Knook with first cord before Thumb; pick up a st in each of 2 marked strands at base of Thumb; remove markers, knit across: {28-30-32}{34-38-40}{42-46-48} sts.

Work even until piece measures approximately {4¾-6-6}{7-7½-7¾}{8½-8¾-9¼}"/{12-15-15}{18-19-19.5}{21.5-22-23.5} cm from foundation ch edge, ending by working a **knit** row.

Next Row: Purl {14-15-16} {17-19-20}{21-23-24} sts, place marker, purl across.

SHAPING

Row 1: K2, slip 1 as if to **knit**, K1, PSSO, knit across to within 3 sts of marker, K2 tog, K1, slip marker, K1, slip 1 as if to **knit**, K1, PSSO, knit across to last 4 sts, K2 tog, K2: {24-26-28}{30-34-36}{38-42-44} sts.

Row 2: Purl across.

Repeat Rows 1 and 2, {1-2-3} {3-4-5}{5-5-5} time(s): {20-18-16} {18-18-16}{18-22-24} sts.

Next Row: K2 tog across: {10-9-8} {9-9-8}{9-11-12} sts.

Cut yarn leaving a long end.

Thread yarn needle with end and slip remaining stitches from cord onto the yarn needle; gather stitches **tightly** to close, then secure end. Weave seam.

Weave in yarn ends ***(Fig. 10, page 38)***.

Variations

Changing Colors

Always start a new ball or skein at the beginning or end of a row, never in the middle ***(Fig. A)***. The yarn can be carried up the side, twisting it every few rows ***(Fig. B)*** or it can be cut, leaving a long end to be woven into the edge or the back of the work.

Fig. A

Fig. B

2-Colors

Work Cuff, Thumb and Hand in Main Color, and Body in Contrasting Color.

Multi Colors

Work Ribbing in Color A, Body in Color B, Thumb in Color C, and Hand in Color D.

Work second Mitten, same as the first **or** switching the positions of the colors, **or** with completely different colors.

2-Color Stripes

Work Cuff in Main Color.

Complete Mitten by alternating 2 rows each of Main Color and Contrasting Color, carrying the yarn loosely along the edge.

Note: The Thumb can be worked solid if the extra yarn ends would make the seam too bulky.

3-Color Stripes

Work Cuff in Main Color.

Complete Mitten by working in the following color sequence: 1 Row each of Color A, Color B, and Main Color, carrying the yarns loosely along the edge.

Note: The Thumb can be worked solid or in stripes.

4-Color Stripes

Work Cuff in Color A.

Complete Mitten by working 4 rows, 2 rows, then 2 rows in any color sequence.

Example: 4 Rows Color A, 2 Rows Color B, 2 Rows Color A, 4 Rows Color B, 2 Rows Color C, 2 Rows Color B, 4 rows Color C, 2 Rows Color D, 2 Rows Color C, 4 Rows Color D, etc.

Multi-Width Stripes

Work Cuff in Color A.

Complete Mitten by working a different number of rows for each color change.

Example: 2 Rows Color A, 6 Rows Color B, 4 Rows Color A, 2 Rows Color B, 8 rows Color A, 4 Rows Color B, etc.

This can also be done with more than 2 colors. To prevent long loops at the edge of the work when carrying color for more than 4 rows, twist the yarns again halfway through the stripe.

Blended Stripes

Work Cuff and Body through Shaping Row 2 in Main Color.

Complete Mitten by working in the following color sequence:

VERSION A

Stripe Row 1: Alternate every other stitch with Main Color and Color A.

Stripe Row 2: Work Main Color stitches with Color A and work Color A stitches with Main Color; cut Main Color.

Work desired amount of rows with Color A.

Stripe Row 3: Alternate every other stitch with Color A and Color B.

Stripe Row 4: Work Color A stitches with Color B and work color B stitches with Color A; cut Color A.

Work desired amount of rows with Color B.

Stripe Row 5: Alternate every other stitch with Color B and Main Color.

Stripe Row 6: Work Color B stitches with Main Color and work Main Color stitches with Color B; cut Color B.

Work desired amount of rows with Main Color.

Repeat the two "blending" rows at each color change. This type of stripe is especially effective when using closely related colors, making the colors seem to "melt" together as in Version A. Version B shows the result of blending sharply contrasting colors.

VERSION B

Gradual Stripes

Start with wide stripes just above the Cuff and gradually work down to very narrow stripes at the finger tips.

To prevent long loops at the edge of the work when carrying color for more than 4 rows, twist the yarns again halfway through the stripe.

Striped Cuff

Note: Always work the first row of the new color on a **right** side row, knitting every stitch instead of working in ribbing. In the following rows, work in the established ribbing. This won't affect the elasticity of the rib unless color changes are very close together.

Knit: With smaller size needles and Main Color, cast on {23-25-27}{29-31-33}{35-37-39} sts.

OR

Knook: With smaller size Knook, ch {23-25-27}{29-31-33}{35-37-39}; pick up {22-24-26}{28-30-32}{34-36-38} sts on foundation ch: {23-25-27}{29-31-33}{35-37-39} sts.

Row 1: P1, (K1, P1) across.

Row 2 (Right side)**:** K1, (P1, K1) across.

Repeat Rows 1 and 2 until ready for a color change, ending by working Row 1.

Next Row: With new color knit across.

Repeat Rows 1 and 2 for desired amount of rows.

Work stripes changing colors in same manner until piece measures approximately {2-2½-2½}{2¾-3-3}{3¼-3¼-3½}"/{5-6.25-6.25}{7-7.5-7.5}{8.25-8.25-9} cm from cast on edge, ending by working Row 1.

Complete Mitten in Main Color.

General Instructions

ABBREVIATIONS

cm	centimeter
K	knit
mm	millimeter
M1	make one
P	purl
PSSO	pass slipped stitch over
st(s)	stitch(es)
tog	together

KNIT / KNOOK TERMINOLOGY		
UNITED STATES		INTERNATIONAL
gauge	=	tension
bind off	=	cast off
yarn over (YO)	=	yarn forward (yfwd) **or** yarn around needle (yrn)

SYMBOLS & TERMS

( ) or **[ ]** — work enclosed instructions **as many** times as specified by the number immediately following **or** contains explanatory remarks.

work even — work without increasing or decreasing in the established pattern.

colon (:) — the number(s) given after a colon at the end of a row or round denote(s) the number of stitches you should have on that row or round.

Yarn Weight Symbol & Names	SUPER FINE 1	FINE 2	LIGHT 3	MEDIUM 4	BULKY 5	SUPER BULKY 6
Type of Yarns in Category	Sock, Fingering Baby	Sport, Baby	DK, Light Worsted	Worsted, Afghan, Aran	Chunky, Craft, Rug	Bulky, Roving
Knook Gauge Ranges in Stockinette St to 4" (10 cm)	27-32 sts	23-26 sts	21-24 sts	16-20 sts	12-15 sts	6-11 sts
Advised Knook Size Range	B-1 to D-3	D-3 to F-5	F-5 to G-6	G-6 to I-9	I-9 to K-10½	M-13 and larger

GAUGE

Exact gauge is **essential** for proper size. Before beginning your project, make a sample swatch in the yarn and needle/Knook specified. After completing the swatch, measure it, counting your stitches and rows carefully. If your swatch is larger or smaller than specified, **make another, changing needle/Knook size to get the correct gauge.** Keep trying until you find the size needles/Knook that will give you the specified gauge.

MARKERS

As a convenience to you, we have used markers to help distinguish the beginning of a pattern. Place markers as instructed. You may use purchased markers or tie a length of contrasting color yarn around the needle/Knook. Remove the marker(s) as instructed or when no longer needed.

Yarn Weight Symbol & Names	LACE 0	SUPER FINE 1	FINE 2	LIGHT 3	MEDIUM 4	BULKY 5	SUPER BULKY 6	JUMBO 7
Type of Yarns in Category	Fingering, size 10 crochet thread	Sock, Fingering, Baby	Sport, Baby	DK, Light Worsted	Worsted, Afghan, Aran	Chunky, Craft, Rug	Super Bulky, Roving	Jumbo, Roving
Knit Gauge Ranges in Stockinette St to 4" (10 cm)	33-40 sts**	27-32 sts	23-26 sts	21-24 sts	16-20 sts	12-15 sts	7-11 sts	6 sts and fewer
Advised Needle Size Range	000 to 1	1 to 3	3 to 5	5 to 7	7 to 9	9 to11	11 to 17	17 and larger

* GUIDELINES ONLY: The chart above reflects the most commonly used gauges and needle sizes for specific yarn categories.

** Lace weight yarns are usually knitted on larger needles to create lacy openwork patterns. Accordingly, a gauge range is difficult to determine. Always follow the gauge stated in your pattern.

BLOCKING

Blocking helps to smooth your work and give it a professional appearance. Check the yarn label for any special instructions about blocking.

With acrylics that can be blocked, place your project on a clean terry towel over a flat surface and pin in place to the desired size using rust-proof pins where needed. Cover it with dampened bath towels. When the towels are dry, the project is blocked.

KNOOKS									
U.S.	E-4	F-5	G-6	H-8	I-9	J-10	K-10 $^1/_2$	L-11	M-13
Metric - mm	3.5	3.75	4	5	5.5	6	6.5	8	9

KNITTING NEEDLES																			
U.S.	0	1	2	3	4	5	6	7	8	9	10	10 $^1/_2$	11	13	15	17	19	35	50
U.K.	13	12	11	10	9	8	7	6	5	4	3	2	1	00	000	---	---	---	---
Metric - mm	2	2.25	2.75	3.25	3.5	3.75	4	4.5	5	5.5	6	6.5	8	9	10	12.75	15	19	25

INCREASE EVENLY ACROSS A ROW

When increasing across the row, the important point is to reach the total number of stitches needed with the increases spaced as evenly as possible.

Add one to the number of increases required and divide that number into the number of stitches on the needle or Knook. Subtract one from the result and the new number is the appropriate number of stitches to be worked between each increase. Adjust the number as needed. Sometimes it's necessary to work more or fewer stitches between increases to arrive at the correct total number of stitches.

■□□□ BEGINNER	Projects for first-time knitters using basic knit and purl stitches. Minimal shaping.
■■□□ EASY	Projects using basic stitches, repetitive stitch patterns, simple color changes, and simple shaping and finishing.
■■■□ INTERMEDIATE	Projects with a variety of stitches, such as basic cables and lace, simple intarsia, double-pointed needles and knitting in the round needle techniques, mid-level shaping and finishing.
■■■■ EXPERIENCED	Projects using advanced techniques and stitches, such as short rows, fair isle, more intricate intarsia, cables, lace patterns, and numerous color changes.

Knit Techniques

INCREASES

KNIT INCREASE

Knit the next stitch but do **not** slip the old stitch off the left needle *(Fig. 1a)*. Insert the right needle into the back loop of the same stitch and **knit** it *(Fig. 1b)*, then slip the old stitch off the left needle.

Fig. 1a

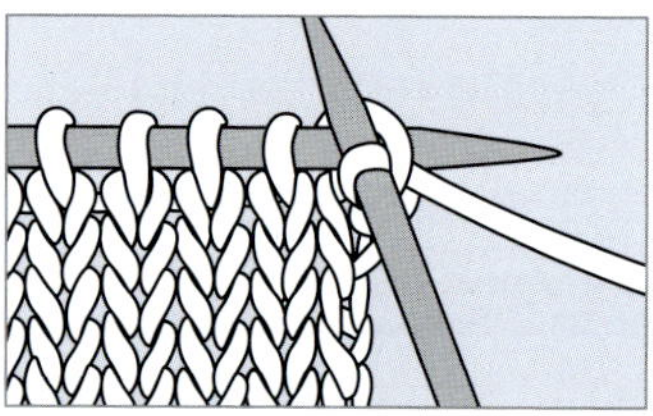

Fig. 1b

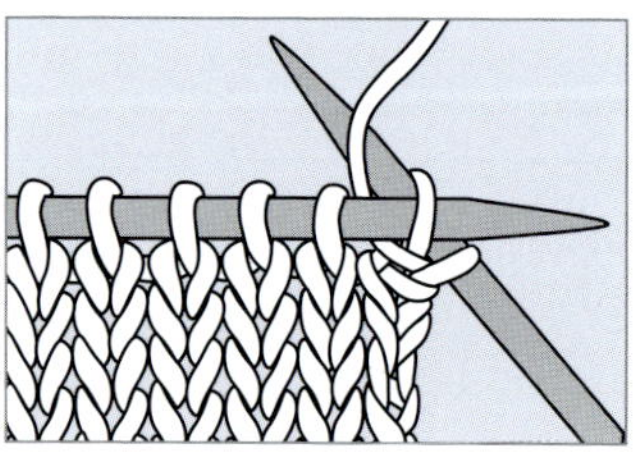

ADDING NEW STITCHES

Insert right needle into stitch as if to knit, yarn over and pull loop through *(Fig. 2a)*, insert left needle into loop just worked from front to back and slip onto left needle *(Fig. 2b)*.

Fig. 2a

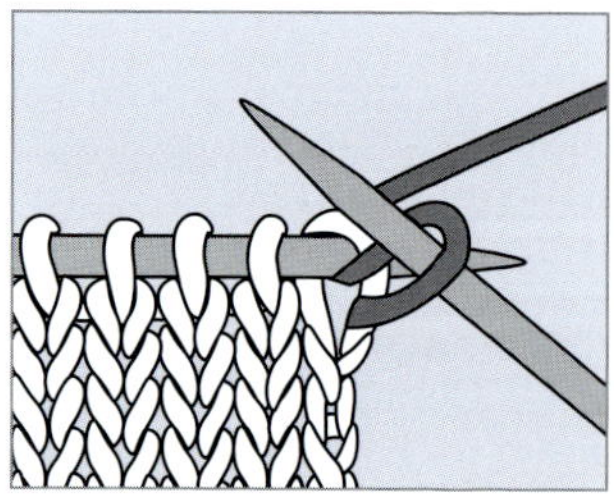

Fig. 2b

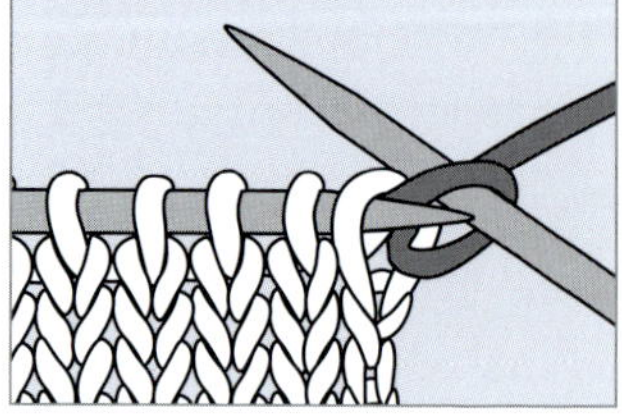

DECREASES

KNIT 2 TOGETHER

(abbreviated K2 tog)

Insert the right needle into the **front** of the first two stitches on the left needle as if to **knit** *(Fig. 3)*, then **knit** them together as if they were one stitch.

Fig. 3

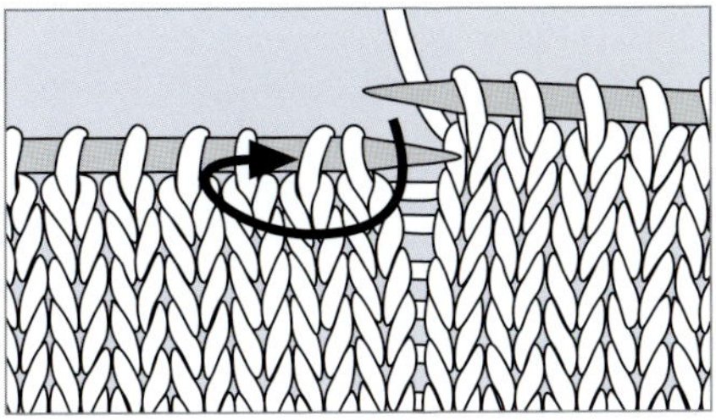

SLIP 1, KNIT 1, PASS SLIPPED STITCH OVER

(abbreviated slip 1, K1, PSSO)

Slip one stitch as if to **knit** *(Fig. 4a)*. Knit the next stitch. With the left needle, bring the slipped stitch over the knit stitch just made *(Fig. 4b)* and off the needle.

Fig. 4a

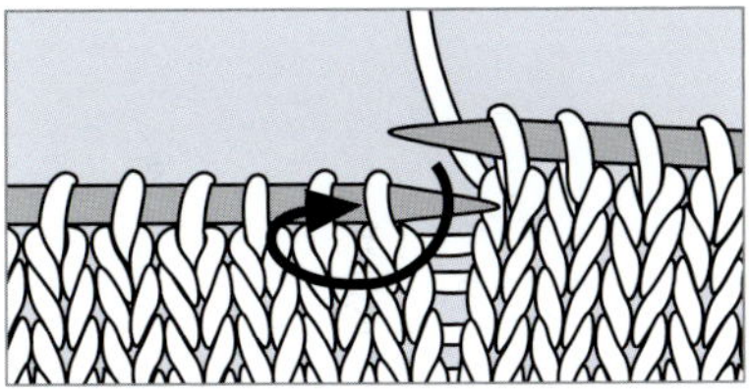

Fig. 4b

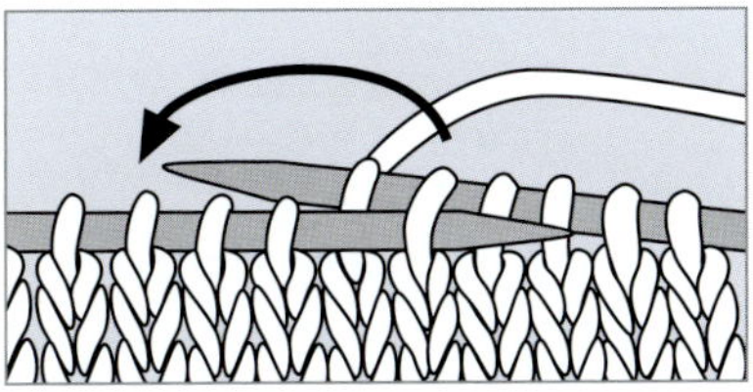

Knook Techniques

INCREASES

KNIT INCREASE

Knit the next stitch *(Fig. 5a)*. Insert the Knook into the back loop of the same stitch and **knit** it *(Fig. 5b)*.

Fig. 5a

Fig. 5b

MAKE ONE *(abbreviated M1)*

With yarn in **back**, insert the Knook under the horizontal strand between the stitches from the **back** to the **front** *(Fig. 6a)*, then knit into that strand *(Fig. 6b)*.

Fig. 6a

Fig. 6b

DECREASES

KNIT 2 TOGETHER

(abbreviated K2 tog)

Insert the Knook into the **front** of the second and then the first stitch on the cord as if to **knit** *(Fig. 7a)*, then knit them together as if they were one stitch *(Fig. 7b)*.

Fig. 7a

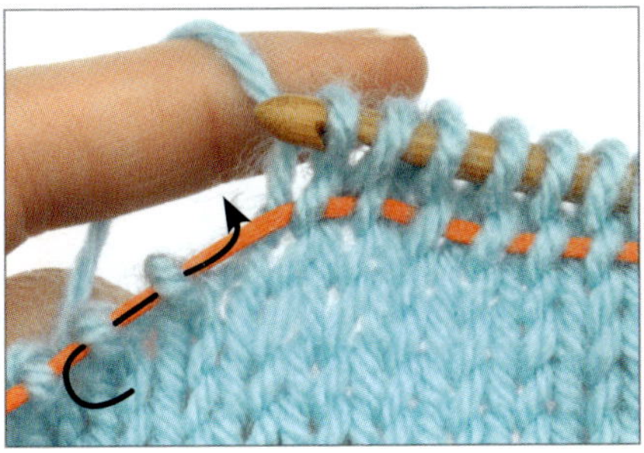

Fig. 7b

SLIP 1, KNIT 1, PASS SLIPPED STITCH OVER

(abbreviated slip 1, K1, PSSO)

Slip next stitch as if to **knit** *(Fig. 8a)*, then knit the next stitch. Pull the stitch just made through the slipped stitch *(Fig. 8b)*.

Fig. 8a

Fig. 8b

WEAVING SEAMS

With **right** sides together and edges even, sew through both sides once to secure the seam. Inserting the needle from **right** to **left**, catch one strand from each edge *(Fig. 9)*. Inserting the needle from **left** to **right** on the next row, catch one strand from each edge. Repeat along the edge, being careful to match rows.

Fig. 9

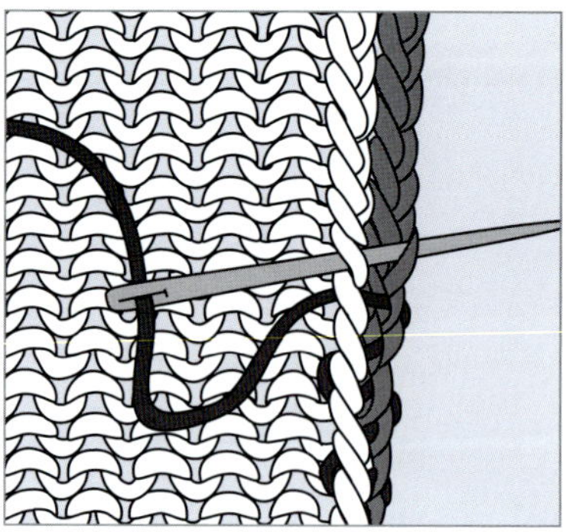

WEAVING IN YARN ENDS

Thread the yarn needle with the long end and weave the needle through the stitches on the wrong side of your piece *(Fig. 10)*. Reverse the direction that you are weaving the end several times until it is securely hidden. Clip the end off close to the work.

Fig. 10

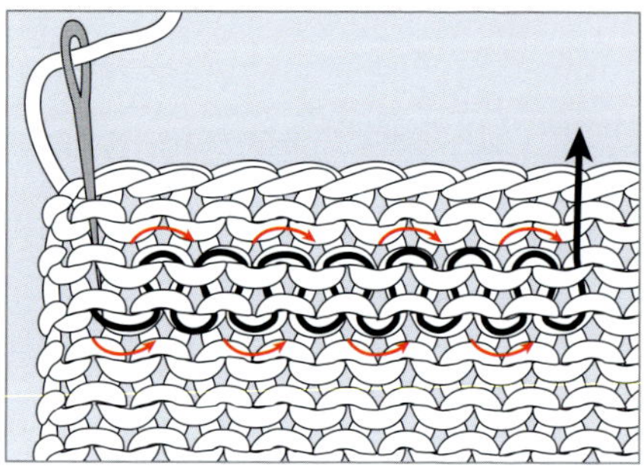

Knit Basics

SLIP KNOT

Pull a length of yarn from the skein. Make a circle on top of the yarn that comes from the skein, allowing a long end of yarn from the end *(Fig. 11a)*. The yarn that comes from the skein is called the working yarn and the other end is the tail.

Fig. 11a

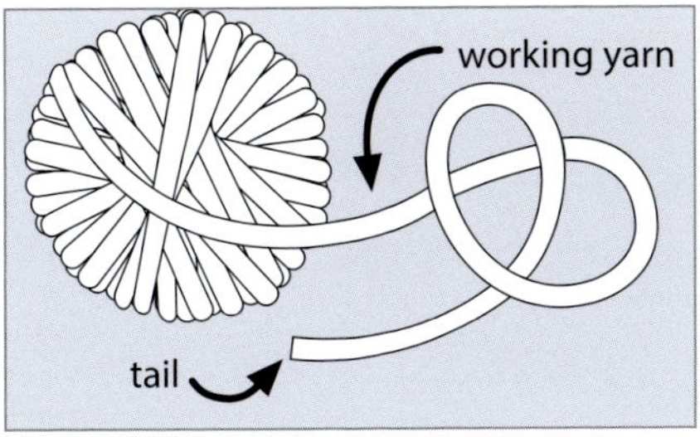

Slip a needle under the strand in the middle of the circle *(Fig. 13b)*.

Fig. 13b

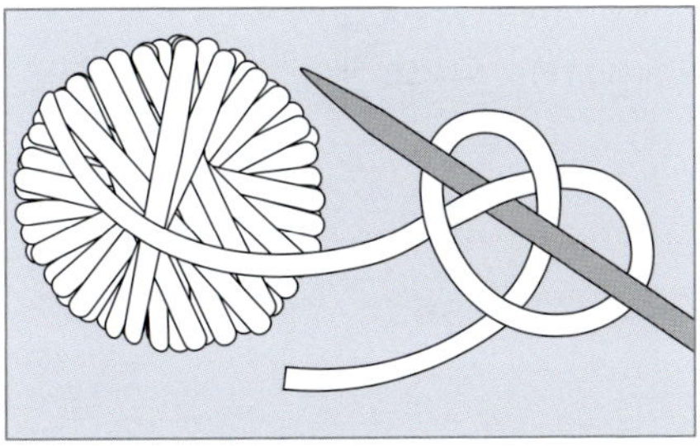

Pull on both strands to tighten the slip knot, then pull on the tail to tighten the loop on your needle *(Fig. 11c)*.

Fig. 11c

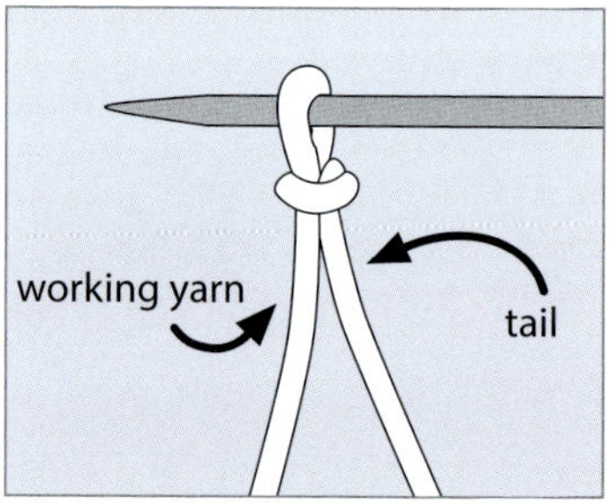

The slip knot should slide easily on your needle. Don't worry if you pull too tightly—you can adjust it by pulling on the strands.

The loop of the slip knot is considered your first stitch on the needle.

SLINGSHOT CAST ON

This is how you put the foundation row of stitches on your needle so you can start knitting.

While there are many different methods to cast on, the slingshot cast on is one of the easiest. Both strands of the yarn are used with this cast on method.

Hold the needle in your right hand with your index finger resting on the stitch. Place the tail end over your left thumb and bring the working yarn up and around your index finger. Hold both yarn strands in your palm with your remaining fingers *(Fig. 12a)*.

Fig. 12a

Insert the needle tip **under** the strand on your thumb *(Fig. 12b)*.

Fig. 12b

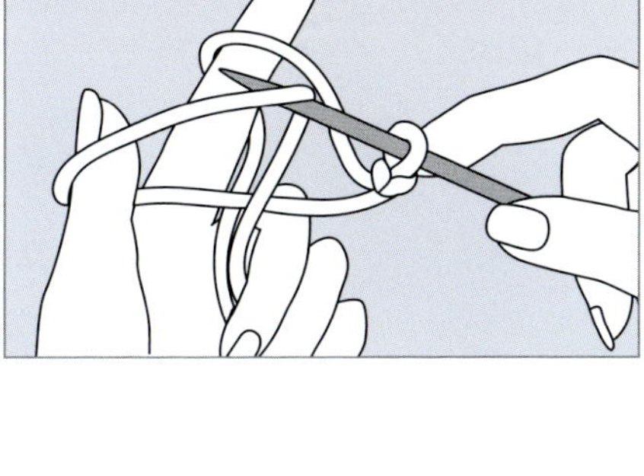

Bring the needle **over** and around the strand on your index finger *(Fig. 12c)*.

Fig. 12c

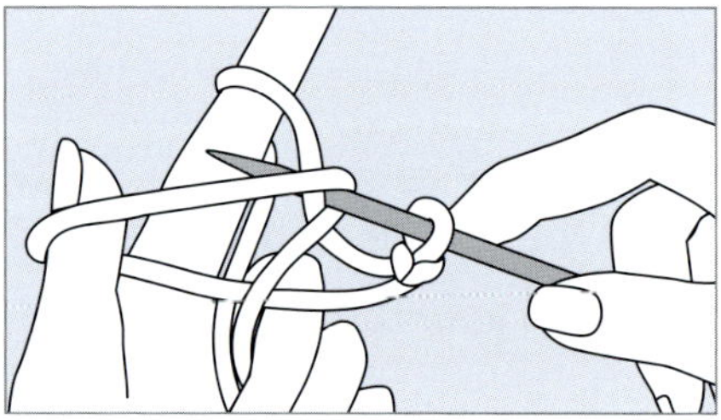

Pull the yarn and the needle down through the loop on your thumb *(Fig. 12d)*.

Fig. 12d

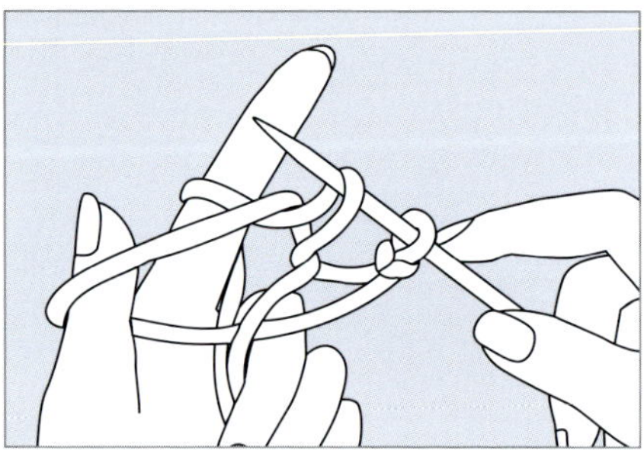

Drop the loop off your left thumb while still holding the yarn strands in your palm. Spread your left thumb and index finger to tighten your new stitch on the needle *(Fig. 12e)*.

Fig. 12e

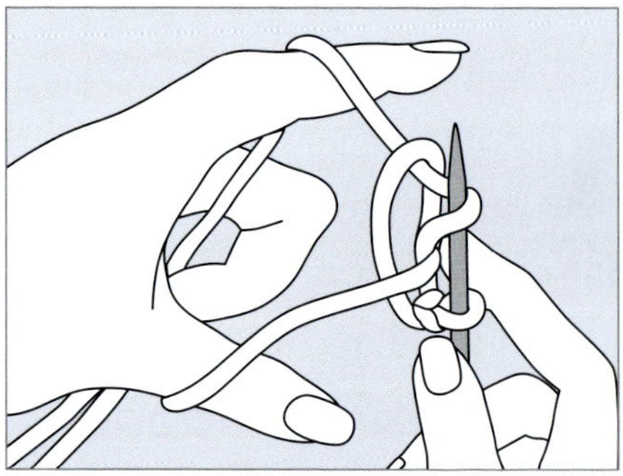

CONTROLLING THE YARN

Wind the working yarn through the fingers of your right hand. This allows you to control the yarn while making your stitches so they aren't too tight or too loose. Then, pick up the empty needle *(Fig. 13)*.

Fig. 13

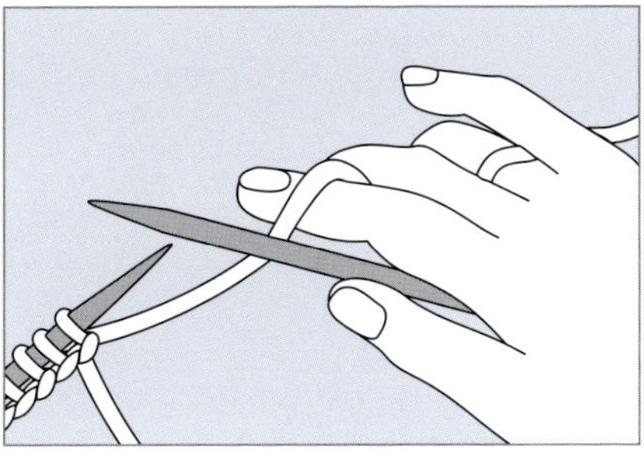

KNIT STITCH

With the working yarn to the back of the needles, slide the right needle into the stitch closest to the tip of the left needle *(Fig. 14a)*.

Fig. 14a

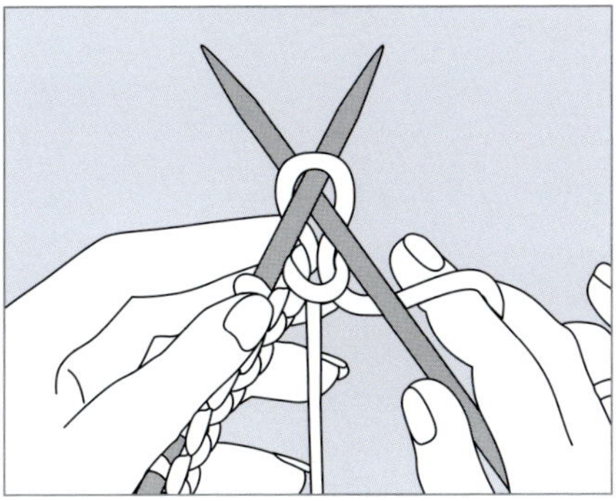

Hold both needles between your left thumb and fingers. Bring the working yarn **around** the right needle and **between** the needles *(Fig. 14b)*, and pull down, tightening the yarn.

Fig. 14b

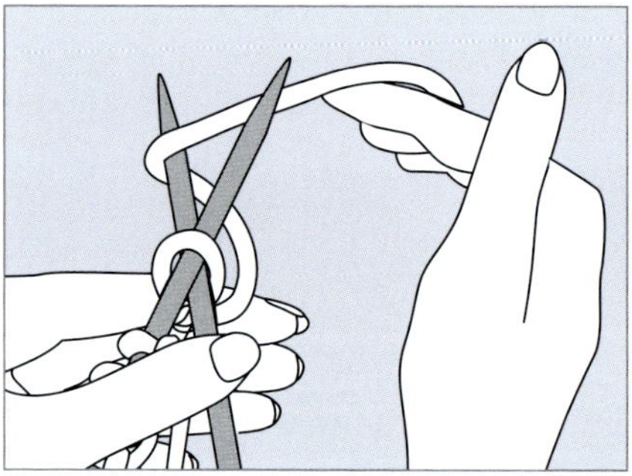

With your right hand, bring the tip of the right needle under the left needle, pulling the loop toward you and through the stitch *(Figs. 14c & d)*.

Fig. 14c

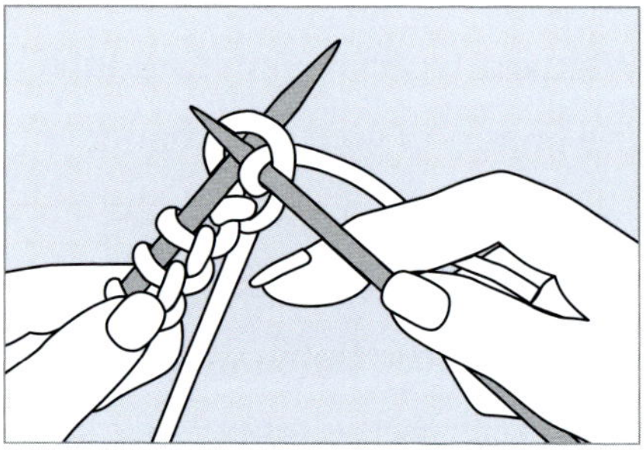

Fig. 14d

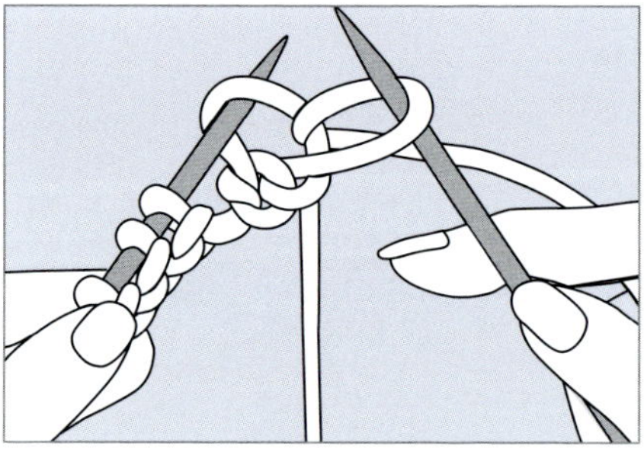

Slip the old stitch off the left needle and tug on the working yarn to tighten the new stitch.

PURL STITCH

Hold the needle with the stitches in your left hand and the empty needle in your right.

Holding yarn in front of work, slide the tip of the right needle into the stitch closest to the tip of the left needle *(Fig. 15a)*.

Fig. 15a

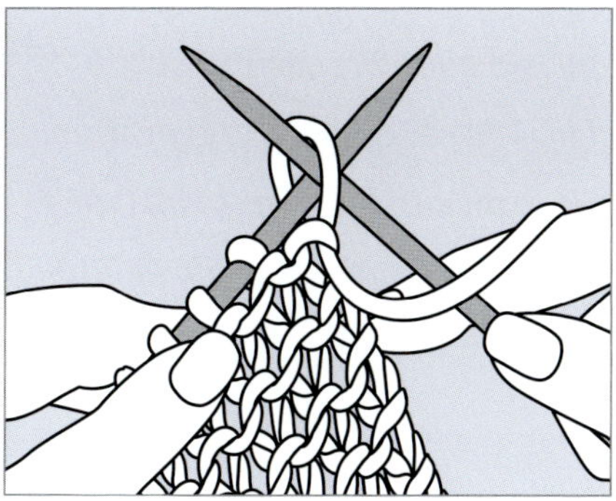

Hold both needles between your left thumb and fingers while you bring the working yarn **between** the needles and around the right needle *(Fig. 15b)* and tighten the yarn.

Fig. 15b

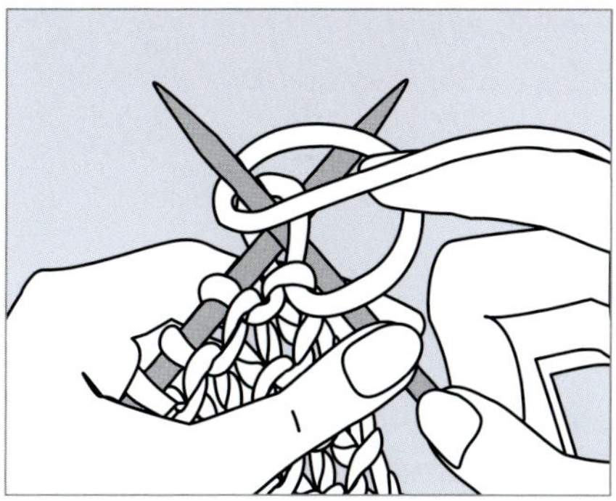

With your right hand, bring the tip of the right needle under the left needle through the stitch, pulling the loop away from you and through the stitch ***(Fig. 15c)***.

Fig. 15c

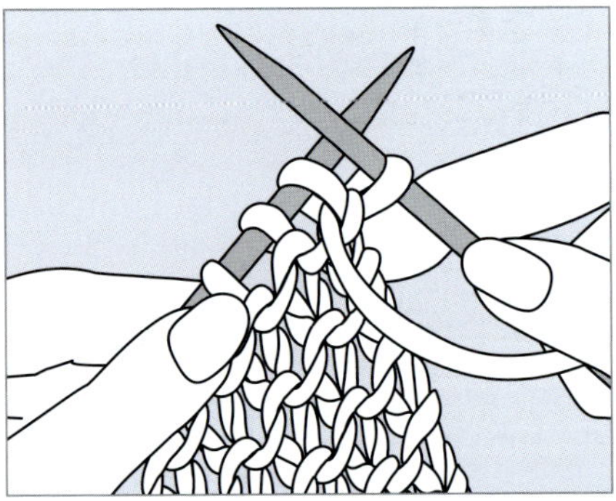

Slip the old stitch off the left needle and tug on the working yarn to tighten the new stitch.

BIND OFF

Binding off is how you remove and secure your stitches from the knitting needles so that they won't unravel.

Knit the first 2 stitches.

Holding the working yarn taut, use your left needle tip to lift the first stitch on the right needle up and over the second stitch ***(Fig. 17a)*** and completely off the right needle ***(Fig. 17b)***. Don't forget to remove the left needle from the stitch.

Fig. 17a

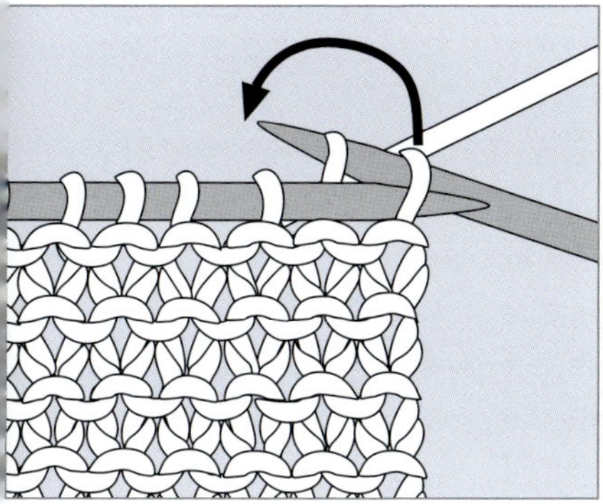

Fig. 17b

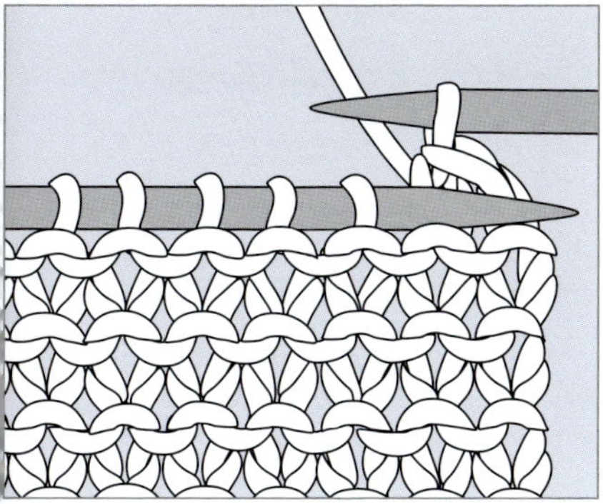

Slip the stitch off the right needle. Pull the yarn end through the loop *(Fig. 17c)* and tighten the stitch.

Fig. 17c

Yarn Information

The mittens in this book were made with Red Heart® Super Saver®. Any brand of Medium Weight Yarn may be used. It is best to refer to the yardage/meters when determining how many balls or skeins to purchase. Remember, to arrive at the finished size, it is the GAUGE/TENSION that is important, not the brand of yarn.

For your convenience, listed below are the colors used to create our photography models. Because yarn manufacturers make frequent changes in their product lines, you may sometimes find it necessary to use a substitute yarn or to search for the discontinued product at alternate suppliers (locally or online).

#0235 Lemon

#0946 Peruvian Print

#3934 Day Glow

#0722 Pretty 'n Pink

#0385 Royal

#0776 Dark Orchid

#0718 Shocking Pink

#0676 Emerald Green

#0966 Cherry Chip

#0512 Turqua

We have made every effort to ensure that these instructions are accurate and complete. We cannot, however, be responsible for human error, typographical mistakes, or variations in individual work.

Production Team: Instructional/Technical Editor - Lois J. Long; Editorial Writer - Susan Frantz Wiles; Senior Graphic Artist - Lora Puls; Photo Stylist - Lori Wenger; and Photographer - Jason Masters.

Items made and instructions tested by Nancy Desmarais and Raymelle Greening.

Made in U.S.A